The author takes you into the psychoanalyst's chamber how hidden psychic in nate every phase of th blistering indictment o is written from sad experience, from the ordeal of struggling against these unacknowledged psychic factors that really control the analysis.

Besides his first hand experience, the author has other excellent qualifications for this expose. For many, years following his analysis, he has represented a group of well known medical text publishers, with the invaluable advantage of speaking to many top flight authorities and keeping abreast of the literature in medicine, surgery and psychiatry. Psychoanalysis lags far off the pace of progress in these fields, while also flouting the ethical standards and practices of the medical profession.

Freud's system is shown to be completely static; frozen in its original design and alienated from all sound scientific procedures and developments. This very isolation has been mistaken for a brilliant innovation to in psychoanalytic incidence are ared of the many harmful results from this unholy marriage of therapy and research carried out at the risk and expense of the patient.

FREUDIAN
PSYCHO-ANTICS

REGENT HOUSE
Publishers
Chicago 10, Illinois

FREUDIAN PSYCHO-ANTICS

Fact and Fraud in Psychoanalysis

BY

MAURICE NATENBERG

REGENT HOUSE
Publishers
114 West Chicago Avenue
Chicago 10, Illinois

1953

CONTENTS

FOREWORD

THE POLICY of inflicting physical brutalities on
the insane has long disappeared because of the work
of the late Clifford Beers and his mental hygiene
movement. Today, however, there exists a new op-
pression imposed in the luxurious setting of the
psychoanalyst's chambers. Instead of a physical,
there is a psychological coercion carried out in the
misapplication of hypnotic and suggestive influences
to further invalid Freudian researches.

It is time for open daylight to dispel the dim
shadows of the psychoanalytic seance; for a piercing
light to focus on Freudian psycho-antics. Free of
regulation and supervision, analysts subject their patients to a merciless observation in the secrecy of
their chambers, keeping them in an introspective
trance for intolerable lengths of time, at exhorbitant
expense, and often with harmful results. All those
considering an analysis should know the influences at
work and the real goal of the treatment. The author
hopes his work will help to that end.

The author also wishes to express his appreciation
to the following for the excerpts quoted in this book:

The Hogarth Press and The Institute of Psycho-Analysis; Perma Giants; International Universities Press; W. W. Norton and Company, Inc.; McGraw-Hill Book Company, Inc.; Random House, Inc.; *American Journal of Psychiatry; The Nation;* and, The University of Chicago Press.

Above all, the author is most indebted to his friend, B. E. L. whose suggestions, help, and encouragement have been invaluable.

CHAPTER I

BENEVOLENT SKEPTICISM

PSYCHOANALYSIS should be learned on the couch; self study cannot entirely reveal its superior attributes; so wrote Freud. I read, believed, and sought enlightenment in over one hundred sessions with an analyst. Then one day, though my reasons were probably vague, I hesitantly requested permission to "quit."

"You can quit if you want to," the analyst quickly assented.

Surprised and pleased with this ready compliance, without further conversation I descended from the couch for the last time, and once outside, experienced a feeling of great liberation. The prospect of ordinary life with the privilege of complete reticence and privacy of thought restored, seemed immensely attractive. Only a gun at my back could force me on the couch once more; of that I was sure.

For several days I reveled in pleasant freedom, but gradually there came a change in mental focus. In retrospect it seemed odd that the analyst did not venture some last word of advice or summarize matters with a professional opinion. It also occurred to me that the analyst had really spoken to me face to face only once, in my first interview. After that, conversation never started until I was on the couch and he was behind it, out of sight.

Through the peculiar introspective haze that had persisted for so long, these thoughts began to come one by one, in a chain reaction. Incident after incident and question after question flashed into my mind until I began to reel with their accumulated effect. Impressions formerly only vague became sharp and clear, enabling me to realistically appraise my experiences on the couch at last. While undergoing them, such capacity seemed entirely lost.

In my disgust and resentment it was staggering to realize the futility and blindness of my experiment on the couch; to finally sense the analyst's incompetence and evasiveness, flavored with his plain animosity. His work had also been the quintessence of doing nothing, for in the first interview he agreed that I needed analysis; in the last he agreed that I could stop; in between he had just sat behind me, listening.

I racked my brain to remember some observation or comment of that Freudian disciple that was indicative of professional competence, or some practical knowledge or discernment. Not only had he never showed these qualities, but also he only seemed, in retrospect, to be interested in concealing his incompetence and lack of talent or skill. It was most disturbing to reflect on my peculiar inability to sense his mediocrity and penetrate through the analyst's pretenses of professional attention.

For a time, these recollections almost completely unnerved me. It was sickening to consider my continuation in those fruitless sessions for over one hundred visits without waking up to the fraud. It was also humiliating to realize that I had to get permission to stop! Because of this very evident paralysis of the will and blindness to realities, I began to think I had developed some nervous or mental disturbance, and the analyst had so quickly been willing to call it quits because it gave him an "out."

Later study and consideration, however, have convinced me that nothing permanently pathological or disordered developed, and my experience could be easily explained in the light of hypnotic phenomena. The prime necessity for inducing a hypnotic state is intense concentration on one idea. This had always been present in my psychoanalysis in my deep absorption with the process of free association. Consequently matters outside the scope of my concentration were hardly noticed and quickly forgotten, which accounted for my overlooking some very elementary considerations.

In this absorption, reactions also became blurred and the memory clouded quickly. I had little capacity to understand the analyst when he did venture some opinion or interpretation, or to evaluate his indifferent efforts for their true worth, or even to realize the implication of my own words. It was a sort of mechanical performance, and at the end of each session a fog of amnesia enveloped everything. But it was free association and my addiction to it that had developed this fog.

Once this haze began to lift, I could see how blindly I had followed the Freudian method of discourse. To me it meant an intensive, introspective search for some all important incident which in recall would bring a complete transformation.

"Free association is like playing a slot machine," I remembered telling the analyst, "You keep on talking until you hit the jackpot."

"Where did you get such a silly idea?" he asked. As usual, this was merely a rhetorical question. If he had attempted to correct this single minded devotion to the free association process, it could have led to revising all my ideas about psychoanalysis. I was still dominated at that time by a poorly digested reading of *The General Introduction to Psychoanaly-*

sis, still captivated by Freud's glibness, his seeming candor, and daring defiance of society. The following passage was particularly haunting:

"We do not require even our patients to bring with them any conviction in favor of psychoanalysis or any devotion to it. It would make us suspicious of them. Benevolent skepticism is the attitude in them which we like best."

"Benevolent skepticism"! This typically glib Freudian phrase illustrates his magnificent mastery of words which created the illusion of his scientific competence. Though it sounds very pretty, the term is self contradictory and really means nothing. Genuine skepticism can hardly be benevolent since it demands proof; unbenevolent skepticism is therefore more consistent. Freud, however, was interested in the benevolence more than in the skepticism, because psychoanalysis requires a modicum of faith.

Once on the couch, twinges of suspicion are suppressed to preserve this faith. This happened continually to me, even in my first conversation with the analyst, making my first appointment. His voice sounded flat and stiff over the phone as he mechanically used a trite phrase probably lifted verbatim from a textbook. The late Dr. Paul Schilder whose fees were beyond my reach, had recommended this analyst as "competent."

His extremely youthful appearance of the collar-ad type, almost femininely handsome, invited no more confidence than his voice. At the time, he looked about my own age—twenty-seven—and better suited for playing the juvenile lead in a Broadway play than the role of healer of sick souls. An obvious amateurishness, made me hesitant about engaging his services, though I did agree to the analysis, but not without mental reservations.

It was really remarkable how I could recall details, once the veil of amnesia lifted. In the next session, in my first few moments on the couch, the analyst interrupted my free associations in the most casual manner, as if his words were really not important.

"You understand that we can guarantee nothing," he said.

I brushed off the impression that his off-hand manner seemed a trifle too studied and could hide an important consideration. Possibly he sensed my hesitancy in the first interview and felt a discouraging condition would kill off any further interest. However, since it is part of the psychoanalytical procedure, as laid down by Freud, to stipulate uncertainties, the analyst had to get it in to complete the record and free himself of any responsibility.

In free association, the patient is extended the

privilege of complete and uninhibited frankness, even to the point of insulting the analyst himself, who allegedly can "take it" in a scientific, unemotional spirit, as material for analysis. In accordance with this principle, I told him one day that visiting his office was like visiting a whore in her professional setting, completely unaware of the truth in this observation or the impact of it on his feelings. Certainly the intimacies of thought in psychoanalysis can be as degrading psychologically and spiritually as the physical intimacies of prostitution.

One day I went even further. After seeing his wife, an extremely attractive woman, I could not help blurting out some rough comments about her sexual desirability. Later I understood why the sessions left me with the empty, disagreeable feeling of violating every tenet of decent reticence. No wonder amnesia developed so quickly after every session on the couch!

Once the preliminary fascination of the seances wore off, I began to realize that I was confiding in a total stranger who had not proved himself. The analyst evaded requests for information about his length of time in practice, his age, the number of patients he had treated and the number he had cured.

"What kind of life would I lead if I had to answer questions like that from all my patients?" he growled.

Once he relapsed into a man-to-man tone, hardly professional, to tell me that one of his patients, a young girl, had misled him about some sexual incidents in a car. At first, the analyst related, he understood only petting was involved, but later he learned that more than just petting occurred. On reminding the girl she had not made this clear in her first account, he said she acted surprised and exclaimed:

"I thought you understoood!"

The analyst related these details in the language one overhears on the street, oblivious to a girl's natural distaste for such brutal disclosures, which had evidently caused her omission. His tone could imply that she had tried to deceive him. It was a most curious self portrayal of incompetence, immaturity and professional insecurity.

Though I could not consciously evaluate these plain evidences of psychoanalytical absurdities, still they registered though only in a dim, blurred sort of way. Since I had started the analysis with misgivings, these impressions undoubtedly accumulated, although it required over 100 sessions for them to materialize.

The most powerful stimulus for dwelling on the value of the analysis came from a total stranger, a cultured, polite individual whose intelligent conversation impressed me. After getting on the subject of psychoanalysis, this fellow admitted trying the treatment, only to have it end when he was no longer able to pay. I then confided to him that I was in the process at that very moment, which was my first disclosure to anyone of this deep, dark secret.

Two conclusions were inevitable from this conversation: Psychoanalysis had not benefited this former patient, while it had been financially ruinous. It was shortly later that I mentioned discontinuing to the analyst.

The words of his assent ("You can quit if you want to.") were as effective as a hypnotist's command to come out of a trance. And my quick departure without asking for a summary or diagnosis was also part of a predestined obedience to a hypnotic suggestion. Since he had "guaranteed nothing," I obediently expected nothing. He also did everything in his power to keep this agreement and that is exactly what I got for my time and money—nothing.

When fully aware of how I had been "taken," I called on Dr. Schilder to give vent to my anger. He was very civil and polite and pointed out the analyst could not have been hostile because of my personal remarks which are received in a professional spirit. He also regretted he could not resume my analysis because of his crowded schedule, which was a curious statement in view of my emphatic, openly expressed aversion for psychoanalysis.

Before he died, Dr. Schilder departed from the narrow paths of Freudianism to formulate his own psychological theories. I have always hoped that my bitter denunciation influenced his decisions, but that is of course only a hope. His dark, impassive yet aesthetic face, was extremely hard to read and masked his sentiments completely as he listened. He was passive in the typical Freudian manner, and his air of detachment seemed to disclaim any responsibility for my sad experience.

To complete the record, I confronted Dr. Schilder's protege at his office without an appointment. He also displayed the strange Freudian passivity and listened without defending himself, as if he were beyond feeling humiliation. As he ushered me out, there was an expression on his face sickening to behold, a half-grin suggestive of sadistic enjoyment. This open display of undisguised emotions revealed more about him than had all my sessions on the couch. No doubt as he sat behind me he had enjoyed my struggles and my very evident ignorance of the real purpose and goal of the treatment.

Both these interviews killed my slight remaining faith in psychoanalysis and proved the inestimable value of direct, face-to-face conversation. I was consoled by one thought—my error was less than the analyst's. I had chosen a bad form of therapy which could be quickly abandoned, but he had picked a debasing career to which he would sacrifice his self respect. At that time he was thirty-six, far older than he looked, and only two years before had studied with Freud in Vienna. I have also learned that he is still analyzing and is considered competent, though he has not attained any high rank in the movement.

My "treatment" is the most regrettable experience of my life and left me convinced that psychoanalysis was pure quackery, inevitably doomed to die. However, as a publishers' representative calling on the medical profession and in constant touch with the professional literature for the past dozen years, I must acknowledge that psychoanalysis is far from a corpse and evidently bears a charmed life. Though the Freudians display no signs of progress and I am convinced my experience is repeated on a greater scale today, people are overwhelming the analysts in their quests for therapy.

Several years ago I was affected again, indirectly, by the brutal administrations of the Freudians and my interest in the subject was revived. A careful re-reading of Freud in the light of first hand experience and genuine skepticism—not the benevolent variety he requested—revealed to me aspects of his discipline which I believe have never been adequately exposed. Stripping psychoanalysis down to its basic fundamentals reveals the real goal and aims of its "therapy." Anyone contemplating an analysis should have this information, for no decision without considering the form and direction that psychoanalysis follows, could be intelligent.

·CHAPTER II

WHAT IS PSYCHOANALYSIS?

THEY SAY there is really nothing new under the sun, but that is probably only half true. There are so many old elements on this earth that they can be joined to form many new and strange combinations. Psychoanalysis is just that—a novelty created by Freud by blending dashes of art, science, religion, philosophy and mysticism. His basic ingredient, however, was just pure authority, an unqualified demand for faith in the reliability of his data which he had gathered from purely verbal communications, and which he claimed could be constructed to form a science. This, of course, radically differs from other scientific disciplines which rely only on the most delicate, precise instruments for measuring and observing phenomena, while Freud received everything only through his ears.

Nor did psychoanalysis develop gradually, for it was created full blown with Freud's publication on dreams. While many branches of science can start with one individual, later workers usually supplement and surpass the originator's discoveries, as astronomy has gone far beyond Copernicus. But in psychoanalysis Freud is still the supreme authority and his system is still exactly as he devised it. None of his disciples have added a single, significant idea to the dogma, nor even succeeded in clarifying Freud's formulations. Dreams still have many different interpretations and no two analysts will interpret the same dream alike. During Freud's lifetime any variation from his teachings was heresy, as Jung, Adler, Stekel, Rank and others quickly learned.

Freud insisted on a separate identity for his discipline and coined the term "psychoanalysis" for association with his name exclusively. "Analysis" was borrowed from chemistry, so Freud implied he had created a method for separating psychological elements. Psychoanalysis is therefore a somewhat incongruous term, for there is no particular connection or relationship between chemistry and psychology.

Chemistry is an exact science whose elements are measured with the greatest precision. New chemical formulas are produced after countless trials and experiments; after proving and demonstrating exact and specific effects. In combining formulas, the demand for accuracy is great because the possibility of error is also great. Errors usually have immediate consequences, which insures a prompt check on accuracy.

Psychoanalysis, however, consists entirely of abstract ideas, gathered and constructed from verbal testimony only. Freud assembled all his data from the conversation of his patients, as they lay on his couch, revealing their innermost thoughts and strivings. Because these disclosures were so intimate, they permitted of but one listener bound by the strictest confidence. Therefore Freud demanded faith from his patient and also from the outside world, since no verification of his original data was possible.

According to his disciples, Freud was an unprecedented genius whose scientific accuracy was entirely dependable and whose intuitive conclusions were phenomenally correct. This made a check unnecessary, think the Freudians, and since a check was also impossible, it was a tight, ironclad system, based on the authority granted Freud because of his genius.

The great man claimed to detect certain common and basic principles of human motivation from these verbal, confidential disclosures. Freud founded his system on the Oedipus complex which he believed binds mankind by incestual ties to the mother and transforms the father into a deadly sexual rival of his son. Since Freud also came to believe that dreams, errors, slips of the tongue, neurotic symp-

toms, phantasies, and lapses of the memory, all had
psychological meaning, this was the material he
worked with. He watched for these mental aberrations in his patients and devised various formulas to
solve their hidden meanings.

This, of course, provides a glaring contrast between psychoanalysis and other sciences, including
chemistry. Freud dealt with nebulous, abstract mental phenomena that could not be measured as can
fractions of a chemical formula. Dreams, for example, can only be interpreted and given some kind
of meaning by employing other abstract concepts.
As is so apparent, there can be a wide divergence in
applying abstract ideas, and dream interpretations
can vary considerably.

"Every dream has many meanings," says Dr.
Thomas M. French in his *The Integration of Behavior* (University of Chicago Press, 1952). "This
fact—one of Freud's first discoveries about dreams—
makes a truly critical attitude toward dream interpretation difficult. Although different analysts may each
interpret the same dream in a different way, this is
no proof that any of the interpretations are incorrect.
Each analyst may have found a different one of the
dream's many meanings."

In other systems, alternate answers to the same
problem are immediately suspected as incorrect, and

there is usually a way of clarifying inconsistencies. Since there is no immediate reaction to a dream interpretation, whether right or wrong, there is no check on error. If a patient's recovery could be effected by a correct dream interpretation, it would be like the workings of a potent drug. A wrong interpretation could work disastrously, producing insanity or an aggravation of the symptoms and an immediate indication of error, as obvious as administering harmful drugs. However, such is not the case in psychoanalysis.

Freudians cannot immediately detect their mistakes and a careful examination of their literature will prove their papers do not dwell on faulty dream interpretations or wrong diagnoses. An air of infallibility, typical of the founder's fanatical belief in the absolute correctness of his method, seems to cloud the Freudian atmosphere. In his self assurance, Freud also insisted his method was scientific.

This, again, was something new, for science has always granted the privilege of doubting all conclusions, questioning fundamentals and demanding demonstrations. Freud evaded all these checks by pleading the peculiar privacy he required excluded outside observers from his chambers. No other scientist or discoverer had ever demanded such a free hand or evaded the responsibility of providing proof. The only witnesses to Freud's procedures were his patients who naturally would not be willing to appear for these same confidential reasons.

Psychoanalysis therefore always had a baffling aspect from its very inception and was so unique as to be hard to describe. Exponents then resorted to analogies and only added to the confusion by associating their methods with well known procedures. It became a practice to point out similarities in surgical and psychoanalytcal principles, as Freud himself often did. The relatives of his patients annoyed Freud with their distrust of his methods and of a purely verbal treatment, and sometimes flatly prohibited his services. In his *General Introduction to Psychoanalysis,* Freud complained:

> "Now ask yourselves how many surgical operations would be successful if they had to be conducted in the presence of the patient's entire family poking their noses into the scene of operation and shrieking aloud at every cut."

In another instance, (*Collected Papers, Volume II*), in his directives on technique Freud mentioned that he permitted his patients to discontinue their treatments whenever they wished. He advised them, however, that this would be as unwise as halting a half-completed surgery. Patients thus ominously warned would not like to imagine themselves with a gaping incision oozing blood, or walking around with exposed intestines, lungs or brain. Freud thus contradicted himself, for this clever and forceful argument prevented unwilling patients from quitting his couch. Such a comparison was also as inaccurate as it was unethical, for there is only a slight relationship between psychoanalytical and surgical principles.

Briefly, these are some general features of surgery: An operation requires the combined efforts of nurse, anesthetist, assistants and surgeon, and can also be witnessed by qualified observers. An operation is not always the surgeon's suggestion alone, but is often made by other physicians after consultation. Later, the pathologist carefully dissects the severed tissue to confirm or disprove the diagnosis. Every phase of the operation is recorded in detail; sometimes photographs, motion pictures, and even telecasts are made as the surgeon works. The incision is kept very small to reduce shock and the surgeon works as fast as possible. He continually watches for errors and takes precautions against them, as stressed in his professional literature. Finally, surgeons depend on an expert knowledge of anatomy, physiology and other branches of medicine.

None of these features exist in psychoanalysis, which is a completely isolated procedure conducted by only one person, who is free of outside regulation and observation. The patient's entire life, his every rational and irrational thought is reviewed, with the danger of damaging sound areas of the personality in such a wide operation. However, the analyst does employ a detached, impersonal attitude somewhat similar to the surgeon's.

Since a surgeon must confine his attention to the diseased parts and to cutting them out, his work is primarily of a physical nature. Psychological considerations would only distract him from his purely mechanical operations. The analyst, however, listens to the highly emotional disclosures of conscious patients. It is hardly beneficial to the patient to listen without responding, one way or the other, to his emotions. Sitting out of sight is a hint in itself that the analyst cannot suppress his emotions. His concealed position gives his motives a tint of duplicity and permits free indulgence in either his warm hearted sympathy or sadistic enjoyment, neither of which are supposed to enter into his technique.

Just as comparisons to surgery and its principles are misleading, so are all other analogies. Freud sometimes compared his unique, unexplainable system to chess strategy, to a detective investigation, or to the Catholic confessional; he also sometimes called it a method of re-education. Psychoanalysis, however, can only be understood when it is judged completely separate from all comparisons, and by reviewing its original roots in the personal idiosyncrasies of Sigmund Freud.

"After forty-one years of medical activity," he confessed in *The Problem of Lay Analysis,* "my self knowledge tells me that I have never been a doctor in the proper sense. I became a doctor through being compelled to deviate from my original purpose."

This vaguely mentioned "original purpose" was the ambition of his student days for pure research. Freud was compelled to abandon years of neurological experiments, and reluctantly became a doctor to earn a living. However, he did not give up his investigative interests, but incorporated speculation and scientific observation and interests into his medical practice. Eventually healing became only a secondary consideration to Freud because of his intense ambition to be immortal.

Throughout his long career, Freud applied his theories to other fields—anthropology, mythology, literature, biography, etc.—and these forays betrayed his real enthusiasms and his grandiose ambitions. In none of these by-paths is a scientific method of proof and investigation imperative, but a persuasive, fluent pen is invaluable. In his self assurance, Freud wrote a work on anthropology—*Totem and Taboo*—

though his closest approach to an aboriginal was through the pages of a book.

Since psychoanalysis is really Sigmund Freud, "What is Psychoanalysis?" can be answered: *"It is his unproven method of psychological investigation conducted under the guise of therapy.* All those who follow Freud and his directives therefore are pursuing the same aims. Current Freudian papers indicate the authors are still primarily research minded, for few bother to discuss therapeutic results and lose themselves in abstract speculations.

A patient in analysis is not told he is contributing both his person and funds to a research project, but is permitted to either believe psychoanalysis is wholly directed towards healing, or that the aims of investigation and cure can be harmlessly combined in one procedure. This, however, is strictly contrary to medical beliefs and practices which require written permission to conduct research on a patient. A surgeon must complete his work and sew up his incision as quickly as possible and limit himself to tried and proven methods. Experiments are conducted only on cadavers or research animals, except under very unusual circumstances.

It may now be understandable why Freud employed misleading comparisons to describe his system for he could not describe it for what it really

was. The influences that he and his disciples brought
to bear in carrying out the hidden, unholy marriage
of research and therapy, is probably the most sordid
side of psychoanalysis. It needs careful, critical examination.

CHAPTER III

THE SORCERY BEHIND THE COUCH

WHEN FREUD entered medical practice, neuroses were new and strange afflictions suddenly affecting many people. At first, investigating these disorders could be condoned because there was no certain method of healing them and much confusion and controversy existed over prevailing methods. This permitted Freud to indulge in his ambition to be a discoverer, a Newton in psychology, for there was a need for reliable knowledge in the field of neuroses. However, Freud looked for new phenomena and did not strive to improve the effectiveness of the best prevailing method of mental healing which was hypnotism and suggestion.

Though hypnotism had achieved brilliant and rapid cures in the hands of competent physicians, the results were not always reliable. It was more an art than a science whose effectiveness was determined by the physician's personality. A dynamic, compelling presence could strongly influence a patient toward health, just as a gifted actor can invest his role with dramatic effectiveness. Freud had just such a personality and before originating psychoanalysis used hypnotism successfully; he obtained rapid cures and was well acquainted with every phase of it.

Because Freud was never a doctor in the "proper sense," his investigative interests led him away from developing his undoubted gift for hypnotism. He not only was never very enthusiastic about healing, but Freud displayed positive reluctance for the physician's role and even a condescending contempt for his patients and their relatives. Nor was his sense of ethics very strong, for otherwise he could never bring himself to stop his patients from leaving his care by employing that gruesome allusion to an unfinished operation.

Freud's reference to relatives "poking their noses into the scene of operation" also revealed his impatience and irascibility. In his annoyance, Freud evidently did not realize these relatives were moved by genuine concern which a physician is obligated to respect. In his preoccupation with research, Freud was little inclined to listen to objections or criticism of his ideas and methods. He was also unlikely to review possible errors, thus he neglected a fruitful source of progress. In short, Freud was temperamentally unfitted for scientific research.

However, he did have remarkable qualities, for he was not an ordinary man by any means. He could and did employ his magnetic, hypnotic personality to advance his own interests by mesmerizing his followers to believe in his genius and to follow him blindly. People who spoke to him invariably agreed on the intensity of his emotions and the piercing look in his eyes. He had the restless energy of a fanatic and a tremendous capacity for literary work. He was linguistically gifted and had a phenomenal memory. As a writer, his style was so readable and interesting that even his absurdities sounded plausible.

Freud's hypnotic personality was quite an advantage in his pre-analytic days. He enjoyed the reputation of being a "miracle worker," since hypnotism worked speedily and dramatically. This speed, however, interfered with his ambition to make new discoveries in psychology which required lengthy and uninterrupted observation. Freud believed in his "right" to investigate his theories of the causes of nervous disorders and justified his eventual abandonment of hypnotism on its poor scientific returns. These statements are based on Freud's autobiography.

Next, Freud became associated with Dr. Breuer, a somewhat older man and a very fine specialist in internal medicine. Breuer also had some original ideas on hysteria and gave Freud a variation on hyp-

notism. After putting a patient into a trance, Breuer
found he could induce him to relate long forgotten
events, bound down by strong emotions. For example, suppose a girl had been seduced at a very early
age and habitually and continually repressed this
memory. By hypnotically removing her repression,
she could be commanded to talk about her unpleasant experience and work off her pent up emotions.

They called this "catharsis" and it worked effectively in curing. Freud, however, did not employ it
for long as he and Breuer became alienated after only
a few years of association. Breuer returned to his
original interest—internal medicine—and never pub-
licly discussed his aversion for continuing in psycho-
therapeutics. Freud attributed Breuer's distaste to the
invariable sexual content of revelations under hypnosis and the emotional attachment patients displayed
for the physician. This, too, was sexually motivated
said Freud.

When the association with Breuer ended, it was
the last regulating agency on Freud's work. From
then on he proceeded on his own to develop psychoanalysis and to stress sexual factors because he said
the disclosures under hypnosis were all sexual. His
speculations then led him to his concept of the unconscious mind, dream theories and dream interpretations.

Psychoanalysis was born with Freud's concept of the dream as a phenomenon of great scientific interest that would lead to the secrets of human motivation. He believed dreams and neurotic symptoms were practically the same and fashioned by the same agency, the unconscious mind. He developed his own method to direct the patient to the same disclosures formerly yielded under hypnosis which he had condemned as unreliable. Though his process was slower, Freud held out the promise of greater reliability in effecting cures. However, since Freud was primarily research minded these cures somehow did not develop, though this promise attracted many patients.

By 1897, when Freud started his school, he had published much and aired his views freely. These views, stressing sexual motivations, were also highly colored by his cock-sure personality and aroused much ridicule, contempt, and aversion, as well as ostracism by the orthodox medical and psychiatric professions. Freud then became convinced that all the evil impulses of society were directed against him, as they had been against Darwin. He believed his discoveries were just as valid as Darwin's and society rejected his theories for the same reason it had evolution—an unwillingness to face the truth.

Freud then was isolated and completely independent of any academic or scientific regulation. He continued his researches and investigations while practicing as a physician. Unofficially, he formed a research institution of his own, "The Sigmund Freud Foundation to Foster Psychoanalysis." Unfortunately, he neglected to inform the world or his patients of this very questionable action. Freud's experimentations, financed by his guinea pigs, is one of the most ingenious arrangements in the annals of human affairs. Not only is psychoanalysis unique, but everything Freud ever did was singular and spectacular.

Freud's technique to carry out his investigations developed from his work with dreams. These were his instructions:

"For the purpose of self-observation with concentrated attention it is advantageous that the patient should take up a restful position and close his eyes; he must be explicitly instructed to renounce all criticism of the thought-formations which he may perceive. He must also be told that the success of the psychoanalysis depends upon his noting and communicating everything that passes through his mind, and that he must not allow himself to suppress one idea because it seems to him unimportant or irrelevant to the subject, or another because it seems nonsensical. He must preserve an absolute impartiality in respect to his ideas; for if he is unsuccessful in find-

ing the desired solution of the dream, the obses-
sional idea or the like, it will be because he
permits himself to be critical of them. . . . As
will be seen, the point is to induce a psychic state
which is in some degree analogous, as regards the
distribution of psychic energy (mobile attention)
to the state of mind before falling asleep—and
also, of course, to the hypnotic state." *Interpretation of Dreams, The Basic Writings of Sigmund
Freud,* Random House, New York, 1938.

This "self observation with concentrated attention"
could also be induced in thinking about other matters besides dreams. The flow of thought formations
arising became known as the "free association of
ideas." If a patient complained of a headache, he
could be asked to "free associate" to headaches as an
abstract idea. Since worries and cares are also known
as "headaches," the analyst's interpretation could be
based on this connection. Practically everything that
comes up for discussion in psychoanalysis is subjected
to this free association process.

The remarkable instructions quoted from *The Interpretation of Dreams,* establish several important
considerations. First, the responsibility for producing
the correct and vital information for the cure was
put directly on the patient and Freud did not actively
seek to draw out the facts. Moreover, by warning
that the "success of the psychoanalysis" depended on

strict conformance to an uncritical attitude and uninhibited expression, Freud allied his aims to the
patient's desire for relief. But most important of all,
hypnotic factors are plainly indicated in the procedure.

Those patients knowing something of Freud's theories on dreams and errors would naturally talk about
these matters, otherwise there would be no point in
submitting to the therapy. Critics of Freud asserted
his methods artificially produced false evidence which
discredited the validity of psychoanalytic conclusions
because of patients' prior knowledge. Freud doggedly
maintained his technique had eliminated prompting
and selection, and even suggestive influences. His
instructions, as quoted, not only belie his denial, but
indicate he created hypnotic conditions to further
his researches.

The revery conducive to producing free associations called for concentrated introspection. Said
Freud, ". . . the point is to induce a psychic state
which is in some degree analogous . . . to the state of
mind before falling asleep—and of course, to the
hypnotic state." This tricky statement both implies
and denies the hypnotic factors at the same time.
Since hypnotism is subtle, changeable and of so many
different shades and depths, it is impossible to see

how Freud could exclude it from his seances, from the "state of mind before falling asleep."

Moreover, it could have been a great temptation for Freud to use the remarkable powers of hypnotism which he knew so intimately. His isolated, ostracized position was somewhat desperate and his early reputation was not favorable. Subjects were not only hard to secure, but harder to keep on the couch for observation. Since magnetism fairly exuded from Freud's personality, it was an inevitable feature of his work and also too powerful a force to ignore.

Patients were also governed by a force—a neurosis—which had the malicious power of disrupting their lives and causing suffering, hence it was to be feared. There were therefore three distinct forces dominating a patient—the neurosis itself, his fear of his neurosis, and hypnotic influences. Freud managed to harness all three of these forces to serve his end. First, he rendered the patient hypnotically suggestible by getting him to relax into a state resembling sleep; then he told the patient that success depended on uninhibited, uncensored disclosures, which permitted the neurosis to exhibit itself in full view. If the patient rebelled he was reminded of his wish to be healed, thus harnessing his fear of his affliction to the process. The patient found no ally in Freud because he was primarily interested in prolonged observation of the illness, rather than trying to halt it.

Psychoanalysis is not only an unwarranted combination of research and therapy, but hypnotism, fear and the motivating force of a neurosis are all maneuvered to subjugate the patient to the procedure. I have shown how these powerful influences worked in my own experience and can also illustrate how they work in the accounts of others who have submitted to the couch. Moreover, every examination of psychoanalysis exposes its basic sorcery—an unprincipled use of psychological influences directed against the emotions or intellect to secure belief and acceptance.

CHAPTER IV

UNCONDITIONAL SURRENDER

PSYCHOANALYSIS became a unique and bizarre way of thinking because Freud was a unique personality. His system is completely individualistic because of his intense egoism, his driving will to power, his inability to serve in a subordinate capacity or endure regulation. Psychoanalysis is completely foreign to established methods of scientific procedure and thinking because Freud could not conform to them. Though psychoanalysis was artificial and different, Freud continually drew misleading analogies to other systems.

Psychoanalysis was developed completely free and independent of other schools of thought in psychiatry, psychology, and medicine, and unconnected in any way with advances in chemistry, biology, physiology, or other sciences. Freud's system is also divorced from anatomical considerations and the "unconscious mind" has never been designated any specific location in the brain or body. Localized functions of the brain which control physical activities are ignored in psychoanalysis. In brief, Freud created his own realm completely isolated from other worlds. His couch became an abyss, a strange, fantastic domain where he manipulated his patients like puppets on strings.

This complete surrender permitted Freud to secure acceptance of all his dogma, particularly the theory of unconscious thinking. To explain the unconscious, Freud dug up another convenient analogy by observing that an iceberg was only one-eighth visible at the surface. The submerged seven-eighths is propelled by hidden currents, Freud said, just as human beings are directed by unseen and mysterious forces. These were, of course, the Oedipus complex and other psychoanalytical "discoveries"—sexual motivations, wish fulfillments, death wishes, castration fears, etc., etc. The unconscious mind thus also served to support Freud's theories and contentions because a patient unaware of these motivations could be told this very unawareness proved the existence of the unconscious mind. It was a vicious circle, kept revolving by Freud's dogmatic personality and his hypnotic powers.

In the admitted practice of hypnotism, it is necessary to secure concentration on a fixed thought, such as the idea of falling asleep. Hypnotism can also be induced by compelling the subject to stare fixedly at a bright object, or to concentrate in various other ways. Dwelling on the introspective idea of "free association" certainly falls within this framework and is more than "analogous to the hypnotic state," as Freud observed; it is that very state.

The hypnotist himself, in his actions, his tone, and in the reliance the subject places in him, governs the depth of the hypnotic state. The subject's emotions, his fear, tensions and wishes, also have some bearing on the depth of the trance induced. The deeper the trance, the more complete the power of the hypnotist.

As is so well known, a subject can be commanded to do many things, with his obedience depending on the depth of his trance and his normal, waking personality. He could cancel hypnotic commands too contrary to his normal impulses. He could not be hypnotized into becoming violent unless he already tended to violent actions.

An unwilling subject commanded to strike someone without provocation could reject the command and withhold the blow, but not without some mental conflict, particularly since he might be ignorant of the source of the command. However, less pronounced actions are easy to command in hypnotism, such as convincing a subject he will not be able to raise his arm, that he will not feel burns, pricks or blows. A subject can be induced to see fantastic objects and to experience illusions and hallucinations. All these are extremely common hypnotic phenomena.

In psychoanalysis, the same features in slightly disguised forms develop; in particular there is a gradual paralysis of the will and an inability to think clearly. Freud demanded a suppression of the critical faculties because thinking and acting on a rational, conscious level did not fit into his technique. Freud immobilized the capacity to reject foolish, irrelevant thoughts, just as a hypnotist can inhibit the ability to feel pain, see normal objects, or perform normal functions.

These ordinarily suppressed thoughts were just the ones that interested Freud in his belief that the unconscious mind was a cesspool of morbid, perverted ideas. His request not to reject these thoughts was essentially a command to express them and people could begin to believe that ideas picked up in the atmosphere of the seance, were actually their own. By pointing out purported evidence of the Oedipus situation, an analyst could inadvertently influence his patient to hate his father and shamefacedly avoid his mother. Every aspect of psychoanalysis, from the agreement that a patient accepts in engaging an analyst, to the theoretical beliefs and actions of the analysts themselves, all reveal the workings of hypnotism.

Because Freud needed docile, willing subjects, he misapplied hypnotism by using it to prolong his treatments rather than work a cure. The same patient, formerly quickly treated by hypnotism and suggestion, was told the new psychoanalytic treatment had greater permanent value though it would take a long, long time. Certainly this, too, is suggestion, employed in this way to prepare the patient's mind for long courses of treatment. By stressing the uncertainties of his therapy in the very first interview, Freud believed he "deprived" his patients of the "right" to protest later on when the results were discouraging. His picture of a neurosis was gloomy and foreboding and gave it the character of a baffling, almost hopeless illness, possibly incurable.

Consequently Freud then found that he not only had few cures to report, but also many failures after long courses. He excused these failures by stressing the difficulties and hazards of his new method which he nevertheless claimed was fruitful of new psychological discoveries and truths. His basic, underlying concern for pure research while being only secondarily interested in therapy, is so easy to read in his directives on technique that it is a wonder of our age that Freud was ever regarded seriously as a healer.

Though Freud admitted his failures were in the "overwhelming majority" (*A General Introduction to Psychoanalysis*) he also claimed he had wrought "brilliant cures" attainable by no other method. For every admission of failure, he usually had some glib counterclaims or excuses, such as his untried, unproven methods, groping in the mystic darkness of uncharted unconscious motivations, etc., etc.

Both cures and failures, however, took a very long time to distinguish and analysis became a long, haphazard affair. In free association the patient was not obligated to dwell on any one subject and could ramble on willy-nilly, as he was struck by new thoughts and associations. For a person unable to concentrate very long on one subject, this was certainly poor training, and the subject was encouraged to talk about anything that suited his fancy. He could dwell on his hopes, fears, grudges, likes, dislikes and the petty events of his life. One thought naturally led to another and he could go on, and on, and on. Freud and his disciples just listened impassively to these monologues, without directly questioning the patient or trying to elicit the information necessary to the cure.

It is therefore understandable why relatives paying for all such conversation, but not under the spell of free association, could get impatient and demand results from Freud. These realistic relatives could also probably see the patient was unchanged, the natural result of allowing complete indulgence in his phantasies and idiosyncrasies of thought. A deterioration in the patient's conditon was also very strongly possible and these angry relatives did not listen very kindly to Freud's excuses, because they were immune from a patient's susceptibility.

Even before consulting an analyst, a prospective patient is somewhat susceptible to his influence. Reading psychoanalytic literature, the recommendations of friends, movies he has seen, can make a prospect curious and even enthusiastic. He will be handled with a technique in his first interview that was so effectively developed by the Master himself that it is almost uniformly followed today. The current books on psychoanalysis reveal this complete dependence on Freud's directives, so cleverly developed for dominating a patient.

Many hostile to psychoanalysis have not hesitated to call it out-and-out charlatanry. The charlatan usually makes glowing promises of a cure, demands a huge fee payable on the spot, and then disappears with his loot after a pretended exercise of magic. Psychoanalysis is different here, too, for the procedure calls for avoiding such tactics and stressing pessimistic prospects and abhoring any definite promises.

Actually pessimism serves their purpose more aptly because promises and assurances can sometimes prove so beneficial that the prospective patient will feel much better and see no need to return. Freud's example called for mentioning uncertainties and difficulties in a vague, general manner, (such as "guaranteeing nothing"). It may be possible that analysts today are sincere in this and ignorant of the reasons for the difficulties in their technique. They may believe that combining research and therapy is not in itself difficult, and in the patient's interests as well as their own.

In the initial interview, analysts usually depend on the prospective patient's own urge to be psychoanalyzed, and they avoid the impression of soliciting. This also serves to transfer the burden of responsibility for success to the analysand. The analysts also avoid agreeing to any definite time limit, and, as a rule, will estimate two years for treatment, though they also add it can run to three, four, or even five years. These vague, dishonest conditions serve equally well to shield shifty, evasive tactics or to hide incompetence.

Today, fees range from about $5.00 to $50.00 per session, with three to five hourly conferences scheduled per week. This makes psychoanalysis a partial-payment plan purchase, but since there is no definite goal or time limit, the ultimate cost is in doubt just as is the ultimate result. At $10.00 per hour and a tentative two year schedule of five visits per week, a patient incurs an obligation of $4500.00, deducting vacation periods.

Financial details are discussed in a cold-blooded, business like tone fixing full responsibility on the patient for his allotted appointments, whether he appears or not. But this exhorbitant financial obligation is not the worst part of the psychoanalytical agreement, or contract as they call it. The patient is asked to invest an overwhelming psychological importance in his analysis that is even worse than the crass material arrangements. All decisions affecting his career, his business, his marital status and love life, or anything else that could interrupt the sessions must be sidetracked until the patient's course is completed.

With free association, the analyst has full access to the patient's innermost thoughts, his most intimate and personal life. For the indefinite period of two to five years, the analyst also takes a big part of his patient's income (unless he is extremely wealthy) and because he demands that the patient combat any important changes in his life, the patient's outside activities are paralyzed. These conditons amount to unconditional surrender, pure and simple.

No other comparable professional relationship has ever existed on this earth. Such one-sided terms amount to intellectual and emotional slavery, and reveal how indelibly Freud placed the stamp of his personality on every phase of his discipline. Only a dictatorial nature could demand such implicit surrender and such absolute authority. Analysts who follow Freud's teachings ape his methods by imposing the same conditions to manipulate their subjects at will.

Since Freudian healing efforts are of an extremely dubious value, these unwarranted demands appear like malicious meddling. However, to make the set-up even more frustrating, the analysts secure the patient's complete dependence and then rigidly refuse to help him in his personal problems. Since his ability to think and act in the cloud of psychoanalytical-hypnotic influences is quite limited, the patient is really in a helpless condition. Since most analyses turn out to be fiascos, the patient not only wastes his time and money, but can also suffer psychological injuries in being subjected to the morbid influences of psychoanalysis.

The pressure of a neurotic disturbance allows no peace and obscures the shoddy, one-sided aspects of the analyst's conditions. They are imposed because the patient's distress renders him desperate. When they are accepted, the patient assumes the entire burden of responsibility and the analyst is only obligated to produce a couch, an office, and his own presence at the proceedings.

The seances begin with this agreement and the analytical procedure calls for only that fantastic method of conversation, the free association of ideas. Actually it is impossible to talk completely at random and in the fashion that Freud demanded. In actual practice, free association requires adopting a completely uncritical state of mind, and once that comes it suits the analyst's purposes nicely. Sometimes the patient hesitates and cannot collect his thoughts to yield free associations, but the analyst will usually sit patiently, waiting for the gush. They have plenty of time—at $5.00 to $50.00 per hour.

If the patient can free associate to some extent (a good many people drop analysis because they simply cannot relapse into the state that induces the proper rapport) he becomes practiced in the art. He can sink into his introspective concentration by merely lying down on the couch, oblivious to the fact that he is indulging in a very expensive way of talking to himself. Often he does just that, for the analyst sits out of sight occupied with his own cogitations. These boring monologues start every hour on the hour in his chambers and the analyst's lapses can be understood even if they are unforgivable.

Because of the expense, absence of beneficial results and the analyst's detached, evasive attitude, common sense sometimes prompts the patient to ask:

"Just where is all this conversation leading? How long must I go on?"

This is a manifestation of the critical faculty that does pop out now and then; it cannot be entirely suppressed. Sometimes the patient will accuse the analyst of not listening and become disgruntled.

The Freudians are well armed to subdue these insurrections; they merely pull the puppet string known as "resistance," a fundamental term and concept in psychoanalysis. Questioning the value of the treatment, coming late for the sessions, wishing to cancel appointments or even drop the agreement, challenging the analyst's interpretations—all these are resistances. According to the Master, these rebellions are the evidence of a negative tendency to avoid the cure.

This, of course, is nothing but psychological intimidation, and resistance as used by the analysts practically amounts to wielding a subjective blackjack. If the patient is convinced that he showed resistance, as he most probably would because of the hypnotic influences present, he further suppresses his common sense. Eventually he can become an automaton spilling out his associations endlessly, and dangling on the analyst's strings, dancing to psychoanalytic tunes.

The patient's docility will eventually become so intensified it can grow into a morbid dependence on the analyst known as the "transference." The hypnotist calls this state the "rapport" in which he can secure obedience to almost any command. Freud knew this as well and instructed that no interpretations are to be ventured until the transference blooms, for the patient can still harbor islands of critical prejudice, resistance or unbenevolent skepticism. Thus the transference arrives after the continual suppression of intelligent thinking in free association has developed into a trance like state.

The analyst then appears under the halo of omniscience and his words are accepted as infallible wisdom. The patient becomes enthusiastic and convinced of the magical properties of the unconscious mind, his own deep sophistication, and his possession of unique and special knowledge. Transferred ones become holy worshippers in all the rites of Freudianism; they recommend it to their friends and acquaintances, write books and plays about it, and give it a tremendous amount of free advertising.

Actually these transferred ones trade stereotyped ways of thinking for sane, common sense reflection. Resistance, transference, super-ego, death wishes and the like, replace words of far greater descriptive powers. Resistance can also be designated as repugnance, aversion, disbelief, chagrin, confusion, discouragement, fear and a number of other reactions, depending on the incidents involved. Psychoanalytical terms are so vague and ambiguous that different ones can cover the same manifestation. What one analyst might call evidence of the negative transference, or hostility to him because the patient rebels at an interpretation, another might call resistance. What one analyst interprets as a sense of guilt, another calls the workings of the super-ego.

Psychoanalysis has always been a fertile field for quacks who have hung out their shingles without training, or what the Freudians call legitimate qualifications. Since the method is so easy to imitate and neurotics are already self-deluded and easy to flimflam, practically anyone can practice the art. It is hard to detect the difference between legitimate and illegitimate Freudians, with or without the proper training. The descent of charlatans into the field is a tip-off on the true nature of psychoanalysis which is so rich with possibilities of fraud.

After reading a few volumes of Freud, many literate, glib sophisticates also become experts on the subject. References to inhibition, repression, penis envy, anal eroticism, ambivalence and resistance, are easy to toss off casually. These psychoanalytical concepts are ridiculously easy to apply on the most superficial evidence and practically anybody can do it.

Suppose an amateur or professional Freudian mentioned the Oedipus complex, the sexual desire for our mothers and wish to murder our fathers. Like the hidden currents directing the iceberg, this complex unconsciously manifests itself in many ways. If you should strenuously object that the concept is absurd, that you never experienced such thoughts, the Freudians have a convenient answer.

They will tell you that even though you were unconscious of the Oedipus complex, it existed in you at one time and remnants of it still exist and can be identified. You need not have been conscious of this evidence. The inference is, of course, that Freudian consciousness of these matters proves them conclusively. If you should argue that you worshipped your father and never hated him and this is foreign to the Oedipus situation, Freudians have another convenient explanation: Our emotions are ambivalent, they say, and have two sides that permit excessive love to conceal repressed hate. In this way, they contaminate veneration and give it the character of hypocrisy to conceal bad feeling.

If you were actually on bad terms with your father for justified or unjustified reasons, you confirm Freud's findings. It is a heads-I-win tails-you-lose proposition. You can argue that your resentment was not based on sexual ideas, but the Freudians know differently and have another pat explanation: The conscious mind gives your hatred other motivations, but at bottom any animosity toward your father was sexually determined and concealed in the unconscious mind.

These are some of the subtleties of Freud's technique, the grand sweep of his amazing deductions that he was inclined to advise could better be seen in the actual analytical experience. Fortunately, this is no longer entirely necessary for one can be guided by the experience of others. Psychoanalysis has such a simple, standardized procedure that its basic elements are easy to detect. Every phase of Freud's system can be discerned in the enthusiastic accounts of two analysands, who have recently published accounts of their life on the couch.

Miss Lucy Freeman, author of *Fight Against Fears,* (Crown Co., New York 1951) spent five years in analysis in which her transference reached a feverish pitch, possibly because of the sex element involved.

She exhibited a typical infatuation for the analyst "John" as she endearingly addressed him in her seances.

The Story of My Psychoanalysis, subtitled "The true and intimate revelations of a man who uncovered the secrets of his unknown self," recounts the experience of John Knight (pseudonym). He spent about two years, 300 hours, and $15.00 per session. His book is a remarkable human document because of the author's excellent education, training, and acute powers of observation and description.

Moreover, Knight was so faithful and conscientious in putting down his experiences and sensations, that his enthusiasm for psychoanalysis in no way detracts from his accuracy. In many instances his account will reveal the workings of the unacknowledged factors of hypnotism and suggestion as described here. Knight's report will also disclose how the analyst employs these influences for his own gain and aggrandizement, in line with Freud's example.

CHAPTER V

A CHEMIST BUYS A GOLD BRICK

"JOHN KNIGHT," author of the revelations from the Freudian couch, cloaks the identity of a man of genuine achievement. He is a qualified scientist, author of books and articles, and enjoys a high standing in his field, chemistry. As a Doctor of Philosophy in his own right, his academic background and education rivalled that of his analyst. Though a brilliant scholar, he is not of the book worm type, for his confessions reveal a warm and human person. He battled hard for everything, not only against the world and against his despotic father, but against his own weaknesses.

The circumstances that brought Knight to the analyst's chambers had an element of coercion. Most usually patients come of their own volition, after reading books and articles on psychoanalysis and diagnosing their own troubles. Knight, however, had been referred to psychoanalysis by his physician, a former Viennese, who had himself been analyzed by the peer of them all, Professor Sigmund Freud.

This physician, a "Doctor Goldschmidt," had been treating Knight's severe stomach ulcer. His recommendation of psychoanalysis was a powerful suggestive factor in itself, for he was an eminent specialist on the faculty of a medical school. His word alone carried authority, particularly since he suggested an alternate and supplementary treatment to his own. He arranged an appointment with a "Doctor Maxwell," the psychoanalyst.

Neither the prospect of helping his ulcer, nor the recommendation of the internist, were at first sufficient to induce Knight to resort to the couch. He only vaguely understood psychoanalysis and to discover what it was all about, he consulted the public library shelves, starting with Freud's *Introductory Lectures*. Knight conceded being impressed by the author's learning, his culture and his scientific approach, which is significant in view of his own academic and scientific qualifications.

Knight was particularly interested in Freud's conception of the libido (the sex drive). This appealed to his scientific predilections, and he compared this libido to the battery and generator of a car, and its correlation with energy, voltage, amperes and resistances. However, Freud's formulations about the libido are just as vague as all his other theories, particularly of the unconscious mind. Knight's idea of this sexual force reveals his own scientific approach and what he read into Freud's nebulous concepts. Like most everything else in psychoanalysis, you can just about write your own ticket and use any comparison with some vague resemblance.

Though Knight accepted this libido theory of sex, he could go no further. When the Master went into his sexual hypotheses, dwelt on castration fears, unresolved Oedipal murderous desires retained since early childhood, and identification of men with mothers and sisters, the chemist simply gagged on it. Nor could he believe in Freud's dictum that our everyday activities were dictated by unconscious motives, "or by complexes buried deep in the subterranean channels of what he calls the Id," (the sum total of instincts and drives.)

Knight's repugnance became deeply aroused, possibly because his training as a scientist and research worker forced him to reject a logic so foreign to his thinking. He could not accept Freud's hypotheses, his terminology or his conclusions. "Passages such as this," he quoted from Freud, "made me think that perhaps Doctor Goldschmidt had been sold a gold brick in Vienna:"

"Fear of castration is naturally not the only motive for repression; to start with, it has no place in the psychology of women, they have, of course,

a castration-complex, but they cannot have any
fear of castration. In its place, for the other sex,
is found fear of the loss of love, obviously a continuation of the fear of the infant at the breast
when it misses its mother . . . you may add fear of
castration, too, to this series, for the loss of the
male genital organ results in the impossibility of a
reunion with the mother, or with a substitute for
her, in the sexual act. I might mention, inci-
dentally, that the common phantasy of returning
into the womb is a substitute for this desire for
coitus."

This quickly cooled off any enthusiasm that Knight
had for Freud. He turned to another tome, Dr.
Franz Alexander's *The Medical Value of Psychoanalysis* and read about the emotional make-up of
ulcer victims. This, too, sounded like gibberish and
he grew weary and perplexed with the riddle of the
interworkings of emotions and body, and sorry he
had heard of psychoanalysis.

This should convey some inkling of Knight's confusion and antipathy, which he faithfully set down
before describing his experiences on the couch.
Though at this point it is hard to believe, later on
this distaste and aversion was transformed into enthusiastic endorsement and worship after succumbing
to Freud's system. Knight's very apt criticism of psychoanalytic concepts indicate his keen intelligence

and critical faculties, the very traits he was later to repress so completely.

Had Knight consulted Freud's autobiography, he would have learned an amazing fact about the man. The Master had been a dismal disappointment in chemistry and the natural sciences in his student days, as he admitted. Freud turned to metapsychology because he could sparkle there with his abilities as a writer, his glibness with the spoken word, and his hypnotic personality. Knight, in his psychoanalysis, eventually followed the teachings of a failure in the very exacting field in which at only thirty, Knight was a success.

As can be seen from the quotation on castration, the thinking that Freud forced on his patients and the world at large is simply unintelligible. So Knight found it, and he was thoroughly dismayed at the idea of being psychoanalyzed and could not stomach the prospect of even discussing the subject in the interview already scheduled with the psychoanalyst. Since there was an available pretext that permitted a trip to New York, Knight cancelled his appointment and flew there on business.

He spent some of his time there pursuing a romance with a woman of mature judgment whose opinion he respected. In his perplexity, Knight questioned her about the advisability of psychiatric treatment. She mentioned the possibility that such treatment might have prevented an unfortunate suicide in her family. After this conversation and just before his plane trip back, Knight suffered an intense attack of anxiety which was frightening. Everything seemed to hit him at once: the end of his romance with this mature, educated woman; his agitation about his ulcer; and his perplexity over psychoanalysis. The attack was so severe and distressing that he wavered in his skepticism. The internist had led him to believe that psychoanalysis could alleviate his ulcer and also possibly dissolve these attacks of anxiety.

Knight then phoned Dr. Goldschmidt, the former Viennese, who laughed about Knight's cancellation of his appointment with the analyst and tossed it off as an evidence of resistance.

"Come back in two years, after your analysis is over," he told Knight, "and I will tell you how I ran away from Papa Freud before starting my own analysis." A new appointment with the analyst was then scheduled.

Powerful emotional and suggestive factors were at work in overruling Knight's original intellectual objections. The pain of his ulcer, the fear of more hemorrhages, the workings of the woman's story of how psychiatry might have prevented a suicide, the strong suggestion of the internist urging psychoanalysis, all combined in their effects. In Knight's own words:

"The resistance had been completely drained out of me by the fright of the attack of anxiety."

It was in this mood that Knight met his psychoanalyst, who majestically overshadowed his patient from a height of six feet four. Doctor Maxwell, the analyst, immediately learned of Knight's anxiety attacks. He then affirmed that Knight needed "some psychiatric help," possibly the full course of psychoanalysis. He suggested that Knight agree to a short, preliminary trial treatment of four to six weeks to determine if the full course would be necessary.

Everything was done in the standardized, Freudian manner, but it is well to consider the emotional and suggestive forces at play in his interesting first interview. Knight had been driven there by fear, his gnawing ulcer, inner turmoil and a desire for relief. His predicament robbed him of strength and power and made his position unfavorable. When two conflicting interests, such as the heads of warring nations, engage in a parley, the one with the better tactical position will naturally exploit it to the utmost. In a peace conference, the victors on the battlefield will do all the dictating; the vanquished will have little choice but to listen.

Knight had put up a rebellion against psycho-analysis by his trip to New York, but the pressure of his anxieties forced him to sue for peace. The analyst knew this and might also have felt resentful about the broken appointment, and one can read between the lines of Knight's account and see almost exactly how the analyst pressed his advantage. Doctor Maxwell immediately put Knight in a suppliant position by observing, almost insultingly, that he needed "some psychiatric help." This is neither a diplomatic, nor pleasant way to express it. When Knight's ulcer was mentioned, the analyst did not promise a cure for it but merely observed that analysts sometimes did work an improvement in ulcers. This vague, indefinite statement could subtly increase tension, since it was far from comforting.

It was not necessary to overwhelm Knight with promises, to seem eager for a patient, or to lead him to expect any miracles. Dr. Maxwell's position did not require him to give any such assurances because of his advantageous position. The analyst merely suggested that the possible resolution of his "difficulties" and the attainment of a "richer emotional life" would be sufficient reason for trying the couch. Knight was only conditioned for an attempt to secure these vague benefits, with the tacit understanding that nothing was guaranteed. It was to be a psychological experiment at the full expense and risk of the subject.

The analyst's commitment was held to the absolute minimum of obligation to produce a benefit. However, though the trial period had not yet started, the analyst immediately broached the matter of a complete analysis, thus suggesting indirectly that the full course would be necessary, and also betraying that the analyst might have discussed it with the internist. Doctor Goldschmidt's cock-sure reference over the phone about returning after two years was a giveaway that even the length of the treatment had already been determined.

The talk about a "trial period" was just bait, to give the chemist a little hope that the complete analysis might not be necessary. Once inveigled into this trial and the subjective influences surrounding the couch, it would then be easy to secure Knight's compliance to a two year course. Doctor Maxwell then also immediately discussed his fees.

When it comes to fees, an air of cheapness, pettiness and unbelievable commercialism hangs over the psychoanalytic arrangements. Analysts discuss the matter of budgets, drawing from savings, and also employ the term "contract" in referring to their agreement with the patient. Knight's negotiations with Doctor Maxwell were true to form in every respect. It did not appear that this was to be a most personal and intimate relationship, with Knight sacrificing his innermost thoughts and feelings on the altar of "science." There was little nicety of feeling or expression. After the terms were arranged over Knight's objections to the time and expense, Doctor Maxwell childishly mentioned that he still had another unused trump card. If Knight had shown further "resistance," he said he was prepared to mention the long years of his training, his financial sacrifices, etc., etc.

The psychoanalytical contract fixed a possible course of eighteen months, more or less, and a fee of $15.00 per session. Unwittingly, Knight had thus agreed to an expenditure of almost $5,000.00, yet the analyst still had the option of calling off the whole affair at the end of the trial period. The practical advantages of such an arrangement are so apparent, that it hardly needs discussion. In this so-called trial period, the analyst can carefully observe his patient's suitability and other characteristics. These are not judged from the standpoint of the patient's needs or from the severity of the ailment, but with a view to determining his docility. The analyst could predict from this trial, any possible trouble arising from a too resistant patient becoming unpleasant after sensing the real implications of a psychoanalysis from many fruitless sessions.

The trial period also eliminates the alcoholics, the vice ridden, gambling addicts, or any others not financially responsible or reliable. Nor do analysts wish to be involved in cases of possible insanity, or relapses into insanity, since they do not know how to prevent such relapses. Psychoanalysts like nice, simple cases, preferably patients of a high type of character, ones that will devote themselves to their analyses with conscientiousness and fortitude and be resigned to a great expenditure of time and money.

Knight was therefore a perfect subject for psychoanalysis. He was young, intelligent and highly suggestible, honest in his obligations and completely independent of family interference. His significant achievements in scholarship and in professional life proved him a strong, sound personality. His anxiety attacks were most probably due to his high strung nervous system and originated from his father's domineering, tyrannical tactics. He developed a definite pattern of behavior from his many brushes with his father and never really learned how to relax. He learned this in psychoanalysis, but unfortunately he also surrendered his customary native shrewdness and intelligence, and was eventually persuaded to go through the entire Freudian procedure.

The technique of psychoanalysis which includes these preliminary discussions with the patient were laid down by Freud after many years of trial and error. The procedures are standard, rigidly followed by psychoanalysts and developed with one dominating idea—to secure subjects for observation. The method is very strong and clever in this respect, but completely lacking in curative procedures and bringing beneficial therapeutic results. Freud's greatest efforts went to securing guinea pigs; once on the couch they were permitted to flounder indefinitely in their free associations. The following quotation from Freud (*Collected Papers, Volume II*) reveals the purpose of warning about difficulties and uncertainties:

> "I hold it to be altogether more honorable and also more expedient, to draw his (the patient's) attention . . . from the very beginning to the difficulties and sacrifices involved; thereby depriving him of the right to assert later on that he had been inveigled into a treatment, the implications and extent of which he did not realize. The patient who lets himself be dissuaded by these considerations would later on have shown himself unsuitable; it is a good thing to institute a selection in this way before the beginning of a treatment.

This is the patented manner of starting a psychoanalysis and certainly Knight's case fell within the usual framework. The chemist's personality is typically conscientious and therefore susceptible to accepting these appalling conditions which can be a challenge. With this characteristic conscientiousness, Knight related his experiences, embellishing his story with authentic details of great psychological and practical value, more instructive than all the collected works of the Master himself. Knight's account was written from the subjective viewpoint of a patient highly gifted and intelligent, and describes all the ramifications of the transference with a clarity of expression that few analysts can match.

The tedious rigmarole and the pseudo-science that makes a mockery of common sense occupied Knight's time for over two years. He "free associated" in the prescribed manner and dutifully reported his most intimate thoughts, his weirdest impulses and irrationalities. Since Doctor Maxwell made no effort to correct or condemn these aberrations, he indirectly encouraged them. Whether Knight's morbidities existed before this analysis, or were engendered in the sticky intimacy of the seances, is very hard to determine.

It is too depressing to go very far into Knight's story which reveals how a really fine mind can be coerced into grovelling at the feet of a mediocrity and making a slavish obeisance for the sake of a "cure." Knight's confessions are of absolutely no scientific value because they were given under duress and in the hopes of alleviating severe anxiety attacks. The analyst at one point even acknowledged forcing Knight into this long, uncertain, difficult treatment. Every detail is complete in *The Story of My Psychoanalysis,* even to Freud's portrait on the wall staring down at the proceedings.

The transference developed according to Freud's precepts, possibly helped by the suggestive influence of his portrait. The huge six feet four of the analyst and his imposing appearance, could most assuredly also help in creating this rapport. While in the throes of it, Knight displayed all the frightened dependence of a child. He was agonized at the thought of a separation and wanted to follow Doctor Maxwell to continue the seances during the summer. Knight's helplessness could also have developed from the analyst's observation in the first interview that he needed "some psychiatric help." According to Freud, transferences arrive spontaneously but this observation of Dr. Maxwell's could have had great effect.

There was a note of whimsical comedy at one point in the proceedings for Knight came to display the typical enthusiasm of the analyzed, once his resistance had been overcome. He did some proselytic work for the cause of Freudianism even while engaged in his amours. He was able to convince a lady friend of the holiness inherent in analysis and she said she would take his place on the couch after he vacated. Both bed and couch would then be kept warm in the sacred devotions to Saint Sigmund.

Knight's story of his treatment also brought out the standardized, indifferent ministrations of the psychoanalyst. It is really astonishing how little this Doctor Maxwell was obliged to do beyond listening. At several points, he ventured some vague opinion or interpretation. At the beginning of the analysis, Dr. Maxwell assured Knight he would be able to recognize himself after the sessions were over. Three months after the analysis was in full process, Knight still showed evidence of resistance by rather critical references to Doctor Goldschmidt, the god-father of the analysis. At least, the psychoanalyst observed that these references were examples of resistance and could be interpreted as "oblique criticisms" of himself. Doctor Maxwell also attempted to allay Knight's worry that psychoanalysis might unduly affect his sex life.

The only instance in which the doctor was aroused to make a really active and energetic effort came when Knight was deeply upset because of an overt display of anti-Semitic prejudice against him. Then this Doctor Maxwell arose in righteous indignation. While he conceded that Knight had some justification he pointed out that his indignation and resentment were exaggerated and when unintelligently directed would defeat Knight's purposes. For some time, said this infallible analyst, he had seen this trait in Knight and could finally contain himself no longer.

This is the only instance in Knight's account that demonstrates the active, purposeful employment of suggestion, as it was used before psychoanalysis. Knight dutifully accepted this criticism, as is only natural in the state of his transference (rightfully the rapport) and quoted instances in his professional relationships where he had profitably applied Doctor Maxwell's suggestion.

However, suggestion was also employed to keep Knight under subjection to the analysis. After eight months, the chemist felt he had received the benefits of the treatment and voiced a wish to end it. Knight was able to attribute his anxiety attacks to their original source—his father's tyrannies which had instilled this habit formation. However, the analyst emphatically refused permission to stop and the course of treatment dragged on for the two years "tentatively" agreed upon in the first interview.

All the unseen, hidden workings of suggestion are plainly apparent in Knight's account because of his accurate, detailed observations. The analysis was long, difficult, and uncertain, just as the analyst predicted it would be, and the free associations were nonsensical, irrelevant and gruesome, because it was implied they should be so. The treatment took the two years the Viennese physician predicted in his phone conversation, and this prediction apparently worked suggestively on the analyst, who prepared Knight for the end after these two years.

Even this was done in the typical Freudian fashion, in a dilatory, wish-washy, indefinite manner. The termination date was set some weeks off in the future, to give Knight time to grow into the prospect of facing life without a psychoanalyst. But Knight was told he could come back even after the treatment was over should he feel the need for further consultations. Knight had been robbed of his independence of thought all during the analysis and this inference that the analysis really never ended displayed a reluctance to restore his self dependence. This gradual process of cutting the Freudian bonds of transference to ease the intense pangs of separation Knight appropriately titled "Weaning."

So ended Knight's "cure," but it is hard to see any glory in it for psychoanalysis. Nor was there any

proof that the treatment had helped his ulcer since
the internist, Doctor Goldschmidt, said it might have
healed without psychoanalysis. Though his account
was written several years after his seances, Knight
still showed their effect. His complete confession of
the innermost secrets of his life went far beyond the
borders of necessity.

The lesson in *The Story of My Psychoanalysis* is
most obvious. It is very questionable whether the
remedy had any value since it disturbed his personality so violently and kept Knight for so long in a
state of intense introspection. Psychoanalysis even
when it heals, appears worse than the affliction, for
the oppressions of the couch are more insufferable
than the illness.

CHAPTER VI

THE INFALLIBLE FORMULA

PSYCHOANALYTIC literature is remarkably free from mentioning errors in diagnosis, interpretation, or the possibility that the Freudian approach and methods could be wrong. This attitude, too, stems from Freud who was always under critical fire and an extremely controversial figure. He consequently did not admit of many errors, for that would provide ammunition for his enemies. He confessed that he was never a physician in the "proper sense" forty-one years after he became one through necessity and his position was somewhat secure.

However, Freud did not believe his reluctance for the physician's role was harmful to his patients. They can best be served, he said in *The Problem of Lay Analysis,* when the physician performs his duty unemotionally and with "precision." His idea of precision, however, is hardly understandable in considering the long, drawn out, inconclusive nature of his course of treatment. At the end of his career, his paper, *Analysis, Terminable and Interminable,* proves

Freud had no reliable method of concluding a treatment. His aversion to considering the possibility of his errors, of the harm and injustice in his methods, is also glaringly evident in this paper.

Most scientific progress has come through constantly checking and re-checking data, from many trials and errors, from consulting experiments by other investigators. Banting's discovery of insulin came through his careful examination of the work of predecessors, basing his own work on their results, and avoiding their errors.

Freud, however, was completely individualistic and his method only led him back to confirming and corroborating his original data and conclusions. The only check on his work, the protests of his patients against his interpretations, was discredited as "resistance." With his concept of the unconscious mind, Freud could attribute any motive he wished to a patient, and with his ambivalence of the emotions concept, he could also convert love into hate to suit his own purposes. The formula was infallible.

Any psychoanalyst who found other methods of interpretation and questioned Freud's theories or absurd formula became suspect. In the days of the Master, these independents could not stay in the movement nor get their views published because Freud controlled the psychoanalytic journals. The same conditions still apply today and those analysts who challenge fundamental Freudian concepts eventually are forced to withdraw and form schools of their own.

Since Freud's method combined research and therapy, the best way to distinguish various psychoanalytic schools of thought is in the emphasis placed on either research or therapy. Freud was, of course, primarily research minded, while Adler and Stekel leaned more to healing. Jung, who became a Nazi during the war, was philosophically bent and probably one of the most devious figures ever attached to the movement.

Stekel was probably the most sincere, able, and least fanatic of the original psychoanalysts. He was concerned mostly with healing and accomplishing results as quickly as possible. Stekel condemned long drawn out treatments and limited his own course to about four months at a maximum. Nor would he treat patients he considered healthy, interested in psychoanalysis as a fad or as a psychological experience. Dr. C. P. Oberndorf is comparable to Stekel in his unflagging interest in improving the record of psychoanalysis in therapy. Freud would probably have considered Dr. Oberndorf a heretic, but he is widely respected in this country as sincere and extremely progressive.

No doubt there are other conscientious psycho-analysts and the willingness to undergo a long course of training is often evidence of sincerity. However, sitting behind a couch is the easiest and most effort-less of occupations, requires only listening, and is de-void of obligation to produce definite, reliable results. It therefore attracts many who are inherently lazy and indolent.

The demand for unlimited disclosures requires more than sincerity and honesty in an analyst. He should be understanding of human problems and character, and have mastered the art of talking to his patients in their own language. By misjudging Freud's temperament and failing to realize his ego-tism and scientific incompetence, analysts appear as unworldly and misinformed. They also narrowly limit their results by clinging so rigidly to the free association process.

Dr. French's *Integration of Behavior* contains a convenient example of the "precision" of current psychoanalytical diagnoses and interpretations. This book is a best seller as the first of a contemplated five volume work and is based to a great extent on Freud. Only two cases are discussed in Dr. French's book, neither of which he treated. He constructed his purely theoretical and scientific formulations from the material supplied him by other analysts. Dr.

French may have occasionally seen one of these two patients, but the actual treatment was the work of one of his pupils.

The other case was treated over twenty years ago in Europe by a famous woman analyst. Dr. French's willingness to base his integrational theories on written material alone, without careful examination of the patient, illustrates another amazing feature of psychoanalysis. Freud was strongly criticized and ridiculed for interpreting the purely fictional dreams of a fictional character in his work, *Delusion and Dream,* but evidently psychoanalysts still follow his example.

Dr. French speculated on the case of his feminine colleague. The patient was a European woman, once famous in her own country as a writer. At about the age of forty-seven, she sank into such a pathetic state of depression and despair, that she was confined to a sanitarium, and three years later treated psychoanalytically. The former writer was obsessed by a terrorizing fixed idea that she would be thrown out into the streets naked, to die alone and forsaken. At times she admitted deserving this miserable fate.

The former writer's life had been one of self sacrifice in the care of a more beautiful sister, eight years younger. When the patient was twelve, her mother died. Nine years later their father died and the older

girl took work as a typist to support her sister, who
was allowed to indulge in some worthless attempts
at authorship. The older girl's devotion to her sister
was marred at one time by jealousy, as she confessed.

The two sisters lived together for "several years,"
writes Dr. French, but then the younger sister married. Somewhat callously, according to the account
in the *Integration of Behavior,* the younger girl left
to live in a distant city. The older sister bore this
with quiet dignity, attached herself to a pet dog, and
lived alone and somewhat secluded. A year and a
half later the dog disappeared and the patient failed
in her frantic efforts to find it, dating her illness from
this point.

The time element is presented so vaguely in this
history that exact intervals are hard to determine.
Dr. French dwelt on the significance of the patient's
composure at her sister's desertion, and the more
acute reaction after the dog disappeared. The second
and more evident upheaval was a delayed reaction to
cover the original disappointment, theorizes Dr.
French. My own conclusion, however, is that the
writer broke down many years after losing both sister
and dog and devoted herself to a successful literary
career in the interval. This, therefore, indicated the
writer had completely recovered from her disappoint-

ment and there were more immediate reasons for
her breakdown.

At any rate, it would appear that the patient could
have been consoled by another dog, or by soliciting
the departed sister's interest in her welfare. Certainly
there was a real basis for her exaggerated terror for
she really was alone and deserted. However, recon-
ciling relatives or finding new pets are simply not
Freudian practices. After the Master became famous
and independent, he insisted his patients be free of
any possible intervention by relatives, otherwise he
would not start an analysis.

Both the original analyst and Dr. French concurred
in this diagnosis of the writer's depression: She had
harbored a death wish for her sister to die naked in
the streets as revenge for deserting her. Since the
conscious mind could not tolerate this deadly wish,
from the mysterious labyrinths of the unconscious it
emerged as a terror of her own death, alone and
forsaken.

The poor woman had not been allowed any real
basis for her fears. In order to be Freudian, her terror
had to be translated into a death wish to conform
with psychoanalytic theories. Just imagine the effectiveness of a therapy based on an attempt to free the
woman from this alleged revengeful motive. The
only evidence of it was a childhood jealously, prob-

ably long outgrown. Her successful literary career proved she outlived this jealousy and her illness could have been due to menopausal factors.

Psychoanalysts do not attempt to directly remove fears and phobias; first they must be suitably analyzed. Once the Freudians select what they think is the correct label for their findings, they believe their job is done. Therapeutic results are seldom mentioned in case histories. *The Integration of Behavior* does not reveal whether the woman writer was cured or became a hopeless invalid.

However, the death wish diagnosis of her case could just as well be replaced by other convenient Freudian concepts, just as dreams can be interpreted in various ways. The Electra complex (the counterpart of the Oedipus complex in men) could easily apply. For example:

When her mother died, the patient fantasied herself as her father's wife and cared for her sister as if she were her child. When eventually her father died, her sister married and deserted her, and her dog also disappeared, the writer imagined all this as a diabolic punishment for her incestual fantasies. Her care, devotion, and sacrifices had been built on a sexual foundation, and in accordance with Freudian theories her illness was an expression of the sense of guilt. As demonstrated for proving the Oedipus complex, the sexual motivations could also be conveniently demonstrated in this case.

Only in the highly subjective atmosphere of the Freudian seance under the sway of the transference, are such diagnoses plausible. In the outside world, these fantastic deductions have been repeatedly rejected as asinine. Yet, this is essentially the "precise" and infallible formula used today in psychoanalysis. A long forgotten childhood jealousy, revived in a pathological state of mind, becomes the basis for diagnosing a severe depression, while more important considerations, such as loss of literary gifts or menopausal factors, are completely ignored.

Such is psychoanalysis.

CHAPTER VII

SHRIEKING RELATIVES

PSYCHOANALYSTS live in two highly contrasting worlds. There is the subjectively colored world of their chambers where the patient regards them with reverent awe and accepts their slightest opinions as Holy Writ. Analysts must also live in the workaday world, earn their livings, justify their procedures, and conform to the standards of the medical profession. They live mostly in their own world; where, from their standpoint, life is more gratifying. Their absolute power must be soothing to the ego, but when analysts emerge from under the halo of the transference to explain their mistakes, they betray effects of this double existence.

Mrs. Dorothy Ferman compelled such emergence and explanation by writing of a tragic instance of failure—"The Psychoanalytic Joy Ride," published in *The Nation* of August 26, 1950. Mrs. Ferman's former husband, the patient, had been an executive in social work and had sought in psychoanalysis a solution of his personal difficulties. He also believed he would arrive at a deeper knowledge of human nature equivalent to post graduate university work and invaluable in his career. Before his marriage, Mr. Ferman had spent some eighteen months in analysis. In line with the agreement, his marriage had to be approved by the analyst, who consented on the grounds it might be "good therapy."

Modern developments can now supply a new slant to fiction writers, In addition to the consent of parents and guardians, analysts and psychiatrists must be consulted for sanction to marriage. Their opinions also carry weight in considering divorces, as happened in the Ferman case. Mrs. Ferman gave the other side of Freud's quarrel with "shrieking" relatives, for her marriage was never free of the hovering shadow of an analyst.

"In our lives there was no mother-in-law, no 'other' man or woman," wrote Mrs. Ferman, "But there was always a psychiatrist." After the first, who had sanctioned their marriage, Mr. Ferman consulted two others in different cities because his profession required him to take new assignments. In seven years there were therefore three different practitioners, and Mrs. Ferman was reduced to the role of a helpless bystander as she saw her husband steadily deteriorate while he was under observation. Mr. Ferman spoke of his long dead mother with childish hate and began to insist that his wife become psychoanalyzed. Mrs. Ferman refused because of her personal distaste for it and the needless expense, and her refusal led to their divorce. Mr. Ferman was eventually confined in a sanitarium as a severe case of depression. A commitment paper was his expected "diploma" for extra-curricular study.

The Nation invited two qualified psychiatrists to comment on Mrs. Ferman's story. One was Dr. Frederic Wertham, the well known psychiatrist, who respects Freud, but does not slavishly follow his methods. He is that rare article, a psychiatrist with a sense of humor, for his comment "What To Do Until the Analyst Goes," was extremely witty. While we have many books of instruction on what to do until the doctor comes, wrote Dr. Wertham, what can be done as analysts are analyzing so interminably and we wait for relatives to be restored to us?

Dr. Wertham sympathized with Mrs. Ferman and thought her complaint well justified; he had seen her tragic experience "duplicated in dozens of instances." Long drawn out treatments are more harmful than beneficial, wrote Dr. Wertham, and thoroughly unnecessary in six out of eight cases. He also commented on the unreal atmosphere of the psychoanalytic seance which compels the patient to live in two worlds and can also give a morbid emphasis to child-

hood memories and animosities. Adult free associations had intensified Mr. Ferman's feeling against his
mother, which had also assumed greater importance
after re-hashing in maturity.

However, psychoanalysts also live in two worlds,
and the second commentator on the Ferman case, Dr.
Gregory Zilboorg, demonstrated evidences of this.
He has written much on psychoanalysis, psychiatric
history, and Freud, and stands high in the councils
of the sect. The tone of his article, "Ignorance, Amateur and Professional," was typically Freudian, dis-
playing all the standard attitudes, including a comparison to surgery. He displayed a slight confusion
about Mrs. Ferman, whom he evidently mistook for
the patient discussed.

"Mrs. Ferman is an unfortunate, unhappy, bitter
person," wrote Dr. Zilboorg. "I follow Frederic
Wertham in his sympathy, but when he joins her in
bitterness, I leave him, for to groan with a suffering
patient is not very illuminating and certainly not at
all helpful to the patient himself."

Dr. Zilboorg's article disclaimed any possibility of
error with the suggestion that, if there were an error,
it must lie somewhere else than in psychoanalysis.
Consequently, he flung his accusations in every possible direction and seized on the possibility that Mr.
Ferman was treated by unauthorized quacks, some-

thing he had not investigated. The education of Mr. Ferman and his daily professional contact with psychiatry as a social worker made this a remote possibility.

Mrs. Ferman had used the terms "psychiatrist" and "psychoanalyst" interchangeably as if they were the same. This indicated her confusion, said Dr. Zilboorg, because of the great difference between the two. However, psychoanalysts were strongly indicated from the terms Mrs. Ferman said her husband employed. If her use of conflicting terms indicates ignorance, then Dr. Zilboorg's publishers are also victims of it, for the cover jacket of one of his own books describes him as a "psychiatrist." It is the psychoanalysts themselves who have caused this confusion, since they also designate themselves as "psychiatrists." However, psychiatrists not identified with Freudianism never call themselves analysts.

According to Dr. Zilboorg's article, the fault lay everywhere except in the Freudian system. Mrs. Ferman was wrong; Dr. Wertham was wrong for sympathizing; society was wrong in causing excessive nervous strains; it was wrong to oversell psychiatry and psychoanalysis (his only admission); and finally the public, too, was wrong, for:

"It takes a long time for the public to become

humble and submit to knowledge in exchange for its garrulous and gullible ignorance."

However, Freud exploited this same "garrulous and gullible ignorance" in addressing his *General Introduction to Psychoanalysis* directly to the public, over the heads of qualified critics who rejected his theories as preposterous.

Dr. Zilboorg also contended the eventual commitment of Mr. Ferman for severe depression indicated a serious ailment and no reliable institution would accept him unless the diagnosis were justified. This inference would also destroy a possibility that the analysts involved were not accredited, for no reputable institution would deal with quacks. Two other questions arise in the Ferman case: Did psychoanalysis aggravate the illness which may have always existed unrecoginzed? Or did the harmful psychoanalytic method create a depression in a normally healthy person?

The trial period in psychoanalysis was devised to eliminate unsuitable cases, though the method of selection seems based on the patient's docility more than anything else. Back in June of 1938, two psychiatrists, (not to be confused with psychoanalysts) Doctors G. B. Jamieson and Edwin E. McNiel, presented a paper at the annual American Psychiatric Convention and discussed the dangers of psychoanalysis for patients with a predisposition for severe mental disorders.

The two psychiatrists had made a detailed study of seventeen psychotic patients admitted to their institution. Every one of these unfortunates had either had analysis at one time, or had succumbed to their psychosis while still on the couch. The periods in analysis varied from two years, with the majority tending toward the incredible duration of seven years of treatment.

"Psychoanalysis had not been of any particular value to any of these unfortunates," said the Doctors Jamieson and McNiel, "and in a selected number had actually precipitated psychosis. . . . The free association and fantasy life without emotional integration tend greatly to lead this type of patient away from reality once he resigns himself to the treatment couch."

The two psychiatrists had the unpleasant job of justifying these seventeen commitments to angry relatives, who were little disposed to listen and angrily mentioned the patients had adapted to life well enough before trying psychoanalysis. Here, again, the investigative side of psychoanalysis and the tendency to regard patients as objects of research could have been at fault. Thinking some of these people were incurable and beyond further harm, the analysts could have dabbled with them to gather material for some esoteric paper.

Since most of these seventeen unfortunates were treated during the depression, they could also have been exploited for mercenary reasons. These ugly facts continually arise, but the psychoanalysts have been able to evade responsibility by glib excuses. Their favorite alibi, à la Freud, is usually: Attempts to uncarth valuable psychological discoveries are justified, even though they fail.

CHAPTER VIII

PSYCHOANALYSTS ON PSYCHOANALYSIS

THIS FREUDIAN inability for proper selection of suitable cases, came up for discussion in a symposium on therapy, published in the *Psychoanalytic Year Book for 1949.* Three well known analysts contributed and their approaches differed widely. Dr. C. P. Oberndorf, whose sincerity and conscientiousness has already been characterized, did not betray any of the fanatic ardor of the typical Freudian in his paper.

Dr. Oberndorf, now past seventy, has had a rich and varied experience and has often been at considerable pains to improve the Freudian record for getting good curative results. His primary aim has always been healing and correction, as evidenced by his many papers on the subject to stimulate the interest of his colleagues in this phase. At times, he has also criticized them for a paucity of papers on therapy and too many theoretical discussions.

Dr. Oberndorf dealt with his own efforts to clarify the picture in therapeutics and gave a dismal report. In 1941 he sent questionnaires to twenty-four leading American analysts who had twenty, or more, years of experience.

"I received eighteen replies," said Dr. Oberndorf, "ranging from simple yes or no answers to a question, to long discussions of the points involved. The replies of these men were very disconcerting. There was nothing upon which they agreed, not on the type of case best suited for analysis, nor results, nor how many patients were helped through analysis to avoid serious mental illnesses. This, of course, added to the already great confusion concerning technique and type of case to which psychoanalysis should be applied."

Dr. Oberndorf also brought out the extremely interesting observation that Freud was always primarily interested in making new discoveries, and only secondarily concerned with "the therapeutic results which might accrue from the theoretically beneficial procedure he was constructing." He also observed that Freud maintained this devotion for research all through his long career and applied his investigative interests to a widening field of studies: anthropology, sociology, literature, art and culture, "rather than specific aspects of medical pathology."

From a conversation with Freud, Dr. Oberndorf mentioned the Master said he did not feel obligated to try to prevent a patient's suicide. The American psychiatrist also observed that Freud retained an iron grip over his disciples and insisted they follow his procedures to the letter. His implication was therefore that Freud's attitude was still prevalent and possibly responsible for poor therapeutic results, and, while Dr. Oberndorf followed Freud in his scientific theories, he rejected his views on healing.

This sincere and able physician also suggested that cases treated for 300 hours or more by psychoanalysis be reviewed in consultation with either another analyst, or a board of three Freudians. He concluded: "Further investigation of the cause for disappointment with psychoanalytic technique is indicated for up to the present time no concerted effort has been made by any group of analysts to pool their experiences to this end."

The second contributor, Dr. Phyllis Greenacre, is a wholehearted Freudian and displayed great ardor for research. She quoted Freud lavishly to support her opinions, and depreciated any tendency for therapeutic zeal in her colleagues. It was indicative of "sadism" contended Dr. Greenacre, as well as "personal ambition," and tended to give the analyst too great an interest in the patient's recovery. Actually this therapeutic zeal is selfish, she affirmed, "for prestige or the feeling of power in curing," and not for the patient's benefit.

She was devoted unmistakably to the Master's principles and opposed to concentrating on therapy to the detriment of research. Yet she displayed the same ardor she condemned in therapy.

"The worker whose goal is the essential verity of his scientific work," said Dr. Greenacre, "may in some instances take unnecessary detours of exploration, but by and large will contribute the most to science and to his patients."

There it is, the credo of the Freudians: Research, first, therapeutic results, later, maybe. Keep in mind her paper discussed living human beings, lying on couches and spilling out the innermost secrets of their most personal lives while paying heavily for an expected cure. An "unnecessary detour" could be dabbling with such disturbed patients as the Doctors Jamieson and McNiel warned should not be allowed to wander in free association.

Dr. Greenacre also said therapeutic zeal betrayed the "naive" lay attitude to expect and believe in the possibility of a cure. The use of the word "naive" indicates that the Freudians believe neuroses are incurable. Freud hinted at this in his *Analysis, Terminable and Interminable* which is his own summary of his work. Analysts also so convinced, are accepting money under false pretenses because patients pay in the hope of being benefited. Possibly analysts believe vaguely mentioned difficulties and uncertainties should convey their treatments are worthless.

The best refutation for Dr. Greenacre's twisted arguments is the fact that Dr. Oberndorf revealed this very therapeutic zeal she bemoaned. Yet he did not display the egotistic, selfish attributes of this un-Freudian viewpoint. Instead, he was humble, though also frankly critical and warned that poor results could be attributed to indifferent therapeutic aims.

The third contributor was Dr. Lawrence S. Kubie, a well known analyst high in the movement. He discussed the scientific aspects of psychoanalysis and said the method was unreliable and unscientific as employed in private practice. Dr. Kubie said the patient's revelations could be distorted by the analyst's own inner complexes and motives. To avoid this distortion, Dr. Kubie suggested using sound recording devices for reproducing the interviews for later consideration, to provide permanently recorded data for review in conferences and seminars.

Dr. Kubie's discussion was very technical and dry, but there was little doubt of his message: Psychoanalysis as privately practiced was not a valid scientific method. He suggested that a heavily endowed research center be set up and staffed by unfettered scientists. Unfortunately, this suggestion arrives over fifty years too late, since Freud should have been so instructed before proceeding on his own.

Summarizing this symposium: One contributor reported that psychoanalysis was unreliable as a therapy; a second said it was not an authentic scientific procedure; only the third maintained her genuine Freudian enthusiasm for retaining the *status quo,* along the lines laid down by the seer of Vienna. Two of three psychoanalysts therefore confirmed what outspoken critics of Freud originally said and wrote many years ago.

Yet this symposium has had remarkably little effect in changing Freudian practices. Only the Chicago school departs to some extent from rigid use of the couch and continued, regular interviews. However, the Chicago group still clings to Freud as the supreme authority and their innovations have not been kindly received by their colleagues. Dr. Oberndorf's dismal consensus is just as accurate as ever, and the current literature of psychoanalysis reveals there is still no significant improvement in the therapeutic picture.

SUMMARIZING FREUDIAN
EXPERIMENTAL ANTICS

In all probability Freud was the cleverest charlatan the world has ever known; a charlatan who succeeded where Mesmer failed. He has endowed his disciples with a technique that is a grotesque mockery of legitimate practice, an experimental caprice that lacks all sense. Research and therapy cannot be profitably combined in one operation because their aims conflict. Research requires permitting a disease to run its course for uninterrupted observation; while therapy demands halting that course as quickly as possible. One purpose cancels the other and combining the two gives—psychoanalysis.

The Freudains are proving that if a patient is hypnotically induced to free associate to the idea of expressing his nonsensical, irrelevant and repulsive thoughts, he will find nonsensical, irrelevant and repulsive ideas to express. Moreover, he will spend a great deal of time and money in the process and come to believe his disclosures have some mystical meaning; that there is sense in nonsense.

Freudians are also only proving their psycho-antics are merely a sort of psycho-anarchy completely lacking in direction and controls. Treatments continue and end haphazardly, directed by accidental influences the analysts are entirely helpless to predict or prevent. The fact that the Freudians immediately mention uncertainties and difficulties, and cannot promise any definite time period or result, shows they are in the dark. Since "uncertainties and difficulties" are their own evaluation of their treatment, the actual possibilities are worse than they will indicate. Overall, a prospective patient has more to lose than to gain in consulting a psychoanalyst, who merely exploits a nervous disturbance and cannot relieve it, and repeats all of Freud's experimental absurdities.